Still Life

"*Still Life* is a vulnerable and brave work. Megan Huwa has faced tremendous difficulties, and in the midst of them, two remarkable things have happened: she has been drawn to Christ, and her eyes have been opened to the dignity present in the lives of other people. These writings are a record of what it looks like when the foundation of a person's faith is tested, and it stands up to the storm."

—MATT WHEELER, Singer-songwriter

"Impressed with tender remembrance and longing through quiet observations that speak volumes about the nuances of life in the face of unexpected weather, Megan's poetry collection, *Still Life*, is a masterpiece of pastoral fine art, imbued with a colorful resilience that compels readers to embrace the human ache of illness while still embodying the intimate details of hope that whisper, 'hold on, pain ends; there is so much more light coming.'"

—ALEXIS LEIGH RAGAN, Poet

"Megan's collection captures the ache of today's brokenness and the hope for tomorrow's restoration. As windows into her own still world, Huwa's picture of a snail or a row of corn slows us to feel our own frailties, yet with a divinely feathered lightness. Her own personal pains are tangible but beautifully submitted to a place where 'grief holds no eternity.' *Still Life* is an intimate story of waiting to be made whole."

—LEE KIBLINGER, author of *All the Untils*

"In her debut collection, Megan Huwa invites us into her *Still Life* which, filled with the specifics of her own experiences, bubbles up a universal desire in us all: that of a life well and fully lived. Huwa's poems are drenched in the wonder of the mundane—sitting in a coffee shop, drawing landscapes as a child, yearly birthday calls—and are there to remind us that tiny miracles are worth savoring . . . even when the unexpected happens, even when pain is also part of our daily lives. From Colorado to California to another world our eyes are yet to see, this poetry collection will take you on a journey that will remind you of what it means to treasure (as the great Mary Oliver would say) your one wild and precious life."

—ROSA LÍA GILBERT, author of *Under the Samán Tree*

"Megan Huwa's *Still Life* is an invitation to a soul-stirring journey. I am deaf and know what it is to struggle with words beyond reach. Yet Megan's vivid imagery and gentle honesty reached me. Her description of farming as 'the art of sustaining life amid the elements' gripped my heart, and the metaphor continues to shape how I face hardship. I've shared these poems with women in deep pain, and holy moments followed."

—DEB ENTSMINGER, Collegiate Initiatives Director, The Navigators

Still Life

POETIC VIGNETTES

≈

Megan Huwa

RESOURCE *Publications* · Eugene, Oregon

STILL LIFE
Poetic Vignettes

Resource Publications
An Imprint of Wipf and Stock Publishers
199 W. 8th Ave., Suite 3
Eugene, OR 97401

www.wipfandstock.com

PAPERBACK ISBN: 979-8-3852-5521-4
HARDCOVER ISBN: 979-8-3852-5522-1
EBOOK ISBN: 979-8-3852-5523-8

To my husband, Jerod,
and my parents, Gary & Brenda Cozzens

Table of Contents

Acknowledgments

THANK YOU, LORD GOD, for being the God who sees, the one who is *so near*, and the Author of my story.

Thank you to my husband, Jerod, who *sees* me, nurtures my story, and *stands by me*, just like our first dance. You are the greatest story and the greatest gift I've ever been given. Thank you for letting me dream and for being my best reader.

Thank you to my parents, who let their tenderhearted farm daughter study an unlikely path in college: creative writing and music. Thank you, Mom, for your unwavering faith in God and for being the first to recognize my knack for writing. You cast a vision for education, including taking numerous writing classes with me over the past 20 years. I still remember you bringing me to your master's courses at the university when I was a small child. Thank you, Dad, for playing George Winston, The Beach Boys, and Bob Dylan, and for your dreaming, creativity, storytelling, and steadfast faith in God despite life's storms.

Thank you to my three older siblings, Ethan, Marcy, & Tyler, who have walked steadily beside me since my first step, and later on, when my health weakened my steps. Thank you, Dad and Mom, for praying for us every morning, raising us on the farmland, and showing us that the greenest grass grows in the valley and the dearest song comes in the night.

Thank you to my in-laws and the thousands of Christians who have prayed and encouraged my husband and me to lean on

God, especially during times of suffering. Thank you for running this race of faith with us.

Thank you to the many writing groups I have led and been part of over the years, including most recently, The Habit Co. Habitation Poetry Group. Thank you to my mom, Lee Kiblinger, Lee Kohman, Joy Manning, and Anna Eastland, who provided feedback during the manuscript stage. Thanks to Jonathan Rogers for helping me discover how my literary writing can synchronize with my faith. Thank you to my endorsers.

Last, but not least, thank you to my fellow shut-ins who press on and press in. I see you, and so does He.

THANK YOU TO THE magazines and journals that first published the following poems:

My First Still Life | *The Habit Podcast*

My Body Language | *The San Antonio Review*

Small Talk in a Loss Universe | *The Clayjar Review*

The Hope in a Scar | *The Habitation Anthology, Vol. II*

Invisible Siege | *Vessels of Light*

Mysterious Way | *Ekstasis*

Life's Stage | *The San Antonio Review*

The Butterfly Pavilion: In the Secret | *The Way Back to Ourselves Literary Journal*

Sanctuary | *The Habitation Anthology, Vol. II*

Dear Woman With a Black Fox-Dog | *The Midwest Quarterly*

Math and Mercy Over Ten Seconds | *The Habitation Anthology, Vol. II*

Counting Stars | *Vita Poetica*

Felt Darkness | *Vessels of Light*

Blessed is She | *LETTERS Journal*

Bare | *Calla Press*

One Hundred Words of Solitude | *Originally published on megan-huwa.com*

ACKNOWLEDGMENTS

Springtime: Two Santas in Street Clothes Meet in a Doctor's Waiting Room | *The Habit Portfolio*

prison's prism | *Foreshadow*

The Sky Above My Bed | *The San Antonio Review*

All, I Prayed | *Calla Press*

A Dream in Response to Words Hanging in the Night Air | *Vessels of Light*

Words too few: It is Well | *Originally published on meganhuwa. com*

The Nursery | *The Midwest Quarterly*

Hymned | *Calla Press*

Imagine a Bird | *Thimble*

While I Wake | *SOLID FOOD PRESS*

Glory, Us | *Foreshadow*

The One Who Sees | *The Habit Portfolio*

Introduction

THE COLLECTION IS DIVIDED into four sections: Shadows, Matter, Witness, and Light. Though my writing often includes weather and seasonal imagery, I did not feel the collection could be split by seasons. I have realized that not everyone gets four seasons.

My story starts young. When my parents dropped me off at kindergarten, they lamented that the world might be too cruel for me. I was a tenderhearted child, the youngest of four children on my family's five-generation farm in northeastern Colorado. While I wasn't David on a mountainside tending sheep, I spent my days building treehouses, helping on the farm, dreaming, and storytelling (including naming everything, like one of our sheep Amy, after I heard that *Amy* was my parents' second choice for my name).

But there is a fall. From a young age, I witnessed the cycles of life, death, and suffering. I observed that in the light, shadows sometimes loomed large on the horizon, yet in the shadows, there would be a sliver of light and the hope of life.

Many years later, during the summer of 2012 at the age of 27, my body was ushered into a spontaneous black hole where all I knew, all I was, all I could do slipped into a void—and I was left broken, weeping in pain every day. Two years later, we found a diagnosis and learned there would not, nor ever, be a quick fix.

So in the waiting, my life involves being still, looking for the sliver of light and the presence of life.

I taught my college students and clients that writing is a powerful tool for exploration, and I have discovered that poetry is a profound vehicle for remembering and beholding. Memories never return linearly, just as poetry is rarely linear. "Only looking back / do I live / in such astonishment" ("While I Wake"), for "there has always been One who has moved across the waters, trading life for life" ("The One Who Sees").

FOUR DEFINITIONS OF STILL LIFE

The term *still life* is used in four distinct ways in this collection.

The collection opens with the poem "My First Still Life," which serves as the seed for the collection's title. *Still life* denotes still life paintings, an art movement that flourished in Europe during the seventeenth century, depicting *memento mori* ("a memento of mortality"). The subject matter encompassed both animate and inanimate objects, as well as rare and familiar items, such as fruit, flowers, and birds, alongside man-made objects like vases and bowls, all of which held special significance for the artist. The viewer is to remain still and behold, engaging in their own meaning-making of the collected objects. Similarly, this poetry collection brings together people and landscapes as poetic still lifes, where the reader can pause and behold life.

Second, due to my health, I am often home and quite literally *still*, managing symptoms. However, being still has become a spiritual posture of the heart. "Be still" in Psalm 46:10 is translated from Hebrew, meaning to release. I hear it as a whisper: *cease striving*. As a farm kid, my work ethic was my identity, so losing my ability to *do* has required me to decrease, release, and surrender to the Author of my life. *Being* with Him is my greatest doing.

Third, *still*ness has developed within me a heart to look toward Life and look for the life around me. I have always been tenderhearted, especially towards those who are overlooked; however, I never thought I would also be living a hidden life due to my health. So, while many poems are about other people, I see myself in them. I think of these as poems of empathy.

Lastly, *still* functions as an adverb in the collection, demonstrating that, despite the circumstances, God sustains and His grace continues.

Nevertheless, *there is life.*

I have tended to these poems like a painter and a farmer—quietly, in solitude, facing the sun and rain, nurturing any life that may break through the soil, weeping at the feet of fall, and reveling in the *life that is* and *lies ahead.*

Anchored upward,
Megan

Shadows

"The sound of colors is so definite that it would be hard to find anyone who would express bright yellow with bass notes, or dark lake with treble."
—Wassily Kandinsky, *Concerning the Spiritual in Art*

MY FIRST STILL LIFE

My initial impression
was red: a poppy field,
a sunrise, an umbrella.

I saw Impressionism for the first time
at the Denver Art Museum
during high school. I knew

little of art except what
my childhood home's west-facing
picture window framed of my

family's farm in Eaton: the milk barn
with wooly ewes in the foreground,
Longs Peak dressed and undressed

in winter's cloak as the background.
Weather was my first encounter
with life's death colliding

sometimes with such resonance,
yet other times with such dissonance.
My dad, the farmer and patient painter,

dabbed the dirt canvas
with small brown seeds
that grew for weeks, months

into swaths of shamrock-colored crops
against a powdery,
puffy blue sky.

I remember summer's betrayal
in July, a storm: Hail pummeled the crops
a disheveling form. My dad

stood at the picture
window with his hands clutching
his sweat-stained Pioneer Seed hat.

Before him lay crops, a hazy
replica of life, and dappled
light striking what I could

barely make out of blurred
shadows cast from the bruising
sky. My first impression

of Monet, Renoir, and Cézanne
at the art museum—though I knew not
their names—was I've seen this before:

broken brush strokes, faded contours,
opposing backgrounds and foregrounds,
and long shadows of still life.

For there is one artwork to marvel:
the steady faith of a farmer
to sow and reap season after season.

My father never disgraced the hail,
nor the drought that hit a few years later;
he waits, still, for a new creation.[1]

1. See Note section for the introduction, *Impressions of a Hometown*, con-
nected to this poem.

MY BODY LANGUAGE

I carry a grief few know, fewer hear—
the language of my body and its foreign sounds:
spontaneous, diagnostic for *no explanation*. It signifies nouns

and verbs external to my state imposing
syntax to my frame. My composition
is a morpheme unable to stand alone.

> One March, I inched across my university's white
> sidewalks to teach the act of writing akin
> to riding a bike. This body of infinitives
> split by the snow so wet it broke tree limbs
> outstretched in premature spring.

> *Just one more step*, I prayed.
> And I heard that kin voice, my older brother
> who taught farming at the same university:
> i.e., the art of sustaining life amid the elements.
> This is a grief few know, yet he saw and toiled with me.

I have read of miracles, yet wonder about my own. But this I know:
grief's sentence is finite, for grief holds no eternity. *Lo*,
witness God rewrite my smallest cry to verb: hands lifted high.

SUGAR CUT

I detasseled sweet corn
one summer: the pull, the pop
not far from my dura's,
the leaves, the stalks
serrating my arms,
the morning dewdrops
leaving me stock-still.

SMALL TALK IN A LOSS UNIVERSE

I dug for verbs
in a dark corner
of a coffee shop
near a Nebula
Award winner
who never saw me,
nor the life,
at the intersection of 11th Avenue.
She made life
in science fiction,
handwritten,
scrawled across
yellow legal notepads.
Her table a hovering saucer,
she, the captain,
and her words
the creatures
of her unfettered galaxy.

That day, like sandpaper
on the tile floor
cutting through
the coffee talk,
a new regular
shuffled in,
his left side
nearly paralyzed
from a farm accident.
In him, I saw my father
emptied
by farming's toil.
With his right hand,
he dropped open
a pocket-lined-notepad

on the counter before the barista.
She flipped through
this farmer's rewritten kingdom.
Then his finger fell
onto these words:
small black coffee.

Now, I am witness,
years later,
to his fettered kingdom,
my own body's
kingdom falling
spontaneously,
displacing me
from my family's land.
Now, I leave
my verbs on the page,
no longer the soil.
Here, I drop my hands open
at a new intersection of mercy.

BLUEJAYS

Heaven's mail comes full-feathered,
  dipping low, untethered, psalming
tierce of grace that makes me whole,
  and as my earth unearths, anabatic winds
compose semitone octaves. Eyes of onyx
  pierce me with a gaze so deep
and a breath so sharp—how could I
  be unmoved by the words
sung on that tree?

WHITE BLANK CANVAS

My mom took up painting
  before my first still-life summer,
and as a little girl, I was transfixed
  by the white blank canvas.
We stood in the farmyard, studying
  the sunset to the west.
Before us, the white-wooled sheep
  bleated. Beyond us lay the fields
of sugar beets, corn, and onions
  tended by my dad. Cottonwood
trees dotted the horizon
  like tiny umbrellas.

She painted, and I beheld
  what stood before me: my mom
painting the horizon. I
  mixed blue and red, painting
a deep purple-sky backdrop. I dotted
  white and yellow stars
in the purple sky. Then I swirled
  the brush in the murky water.
On the palette, I mopped up
  yellow paint, and across
the purple sky, I painted
  a yellow heart that touched from
end to end to end to end.

It wasn't the landscape,
  but I painted what I witnessed.

ON DESIRE & DELIGHT

Someone else's peace lily grows in the ferns
    by our front door, but in its place,
I've desired hydrangeas. Expectant
    more than once of a pink or blue debut
in spring, I've poured pitcher after pitcher
    on the shaded bed. *(May you drown
with delight in the water.)* But the shade
    has offered little color of life, only night-
singed leaves and sepia-veined blooms.

But today, I lock the door behind me,
    glancing the lily's heart-shaped leaves breaking
from the soldiered ferns, reaching to me as
    though it knows another's sorrow in the
shadow. The ferns soldier on while
    in the umbra, the peace lily dwells,
delighting in the water,
    listening to the whisper,
        looking for life among the living—
            or the just beginning.

WEATHER & PARAPHRASE

My parents call every birthday,
   and my dad gives the weather
report (because we don't feel
   the same weather anymore):
"Sunny skies"—and I picture him
   with eyes fixed on my mom—
"A second summer
   like when you were born."

My mom tells the story:
   I arrived right before lunch,
and thanks be to God
   because, "I lost a lot of blood."
I was the last of four children,
   and I can't imagine her release.

Then praises for life ascend—
   hers and mine. Perhaps that's why
I have stuck so close to her
   with my words. My life
is a paraphrase of hers.

INVISIBLE SIEGE

I exhale in white space
1,200 miles from home
and grieve this mimicry of life
where ink-black font overlays
artificial white. I am a fleck
of dust blown from the binding of a book—

   a free fall,
   invisible,
   swarmed
   by unknown flecks,
   until light breaks through
   the open window:

      the light transfigures light,
      the speck becomes matter,
      the matter matters,
      the free falls with might.

THE BEST DRAWING OF RURAL LIFE

I learned to draw a partly sunny sky in first grade.
I drew what I knew in color:

my dad in a tractor discing brown soil
with green sweet corn growing in the field

and barn swallows flying in an open, sunny sky.
Then I saw Will's partly cloudy sky—

rays hid behind a thick cloud that hung low.
The cloud traveled across his sun,

and what I thought were raindrops falling
were bits of eraser raining down—his eraser black

in his hand, his sunny sky turned cloudy.
I erased a sliver of my sun and added a cloud,

connecting arc to arc until my ends met.
When the teacher wasn't looking, Will folded his drawing

into a paper airplane and threw it across the room.
        (This is what I want to remember about Will.)

My rural life drawing won second place and publication
in *The Tribune*, but all I could think was

my partly cloudy sky was Will's sky, not mine.
Because some life drawings have cloudy skies,

some are in color,
and some are spun

into paper airplanes to see
whose life flies the farthest.

THE HOPE IN A SCAR

A staggering stature, he takes communion,
then crushes the plastic cup.

And I glimpse to see if his palms are scarred red,
but he hurries back to his pew
as though communion is just him and Jesus.

A month later, he steps into the waters,
a staggering stature beneath the stained glass of Jesus.

The pastor dips him back into the water,
and his palms clench the glass of the baptistry—
    the waters may overtake him.

So with bent knees, his head above water,
he and the pastor count *three, two, one.*
His legs give way, and the waters wash over him.

He rises, waves his unblemished hand,
and we cheer him to a new life.

MYSTERIOUS WAY

The ring of January is not glee
running wild, free with whole-hearted jubilee.
Its vacancy is hushed and draped white,
its hope is hidden beneath the cloak of might
that new life is mustering its courage,
neath the weighty cloak, to emerge
in March, April, or May. And may it be—

So I walk with William Cowper's verse in my ear
and tack to and fro our neighborhood near.
This day, every day, every door the same
except a violin—*Theme of Schindler's List*—
has through a cracked front door slipped.

The sound of sorrow practiced over and again;
one whose violin grieves like Cowper's pen.
Minutes pass and I am still standing,
for this theme is no orchestra playing;
it is one embodied—
one with bow in hand, body upon
the shoulder beneath the chin,
bowing an immutable ghost note

With the sun anchored upward,
I turn to tack home,
taken by why
my shadow is so long
and how the sun still shines.

Matter

Chords that were broken will vibrate once more.
—*Fanny J. Crosby*, "Rescue the Perishing"

LIFE'S STAGE

This one window stages the little girl two doors down, alone
in the grass with a purple-casted hand and a pink ball.
She tosses one, two, three, four against the stucco wall.
Could I catch her and say, though your dad's temper is your only
friend, you're not alone?

This same window stages the depressed next-door neighbor,
who slips across the stage at day's end,
whose texts read as a script: *I need a friend.*
I respond: *I'm here,* hoping brevity echoes despair.

This window stages the middle-aged man down the street
whose labored steps are often pitied by the able.
I don't know his tragedy but I know mine, and I want to whisper these
syllables: Your step is noble, triumphant—a feat.

For life's tragedy is when you see it but you do not feel it,
when empathy's wind drums against the window:
> *Open.* Though the night is dim, it's still moonlit;
> though the chorus is faint, our words cannot go unspoken.

THE BUTTERFLY PAVILION: IN THE SECRET

Who do you carry with you? I wondered,
      in smothering humidity, where weightless
winged nobility hovered above us.
        You knelt at the eucalyptus tree's roots,

in smothering humidity, where weightless,
      I hid behind Bird of Paradise, beholding.
You knelt at the eucalyptus tree's roots,
        and scattered loose ashes from a marble jar.

I hid behind Bird of Paradise, beholding
      you murmur to the roots words unheard,
scattered loose like ashes from a marble jar.
        Your fingers combed the ashes around the tree,

whispering to the roots words unheard:
      the dead language of lament.
Your fingers combed the echoes around the tree—
           may I carry you with me?

CONSOLATION SHOWER

for M

That night, we spoke
of things unspeakable:

cancer, aging, our bodies failing
at too young an age.

We celebrated your life
was not taken, my frame

unmistaken before a fountain,
showering us shook

with straying mist and
lights beaming high

to the star-laden sky.
In verse, one man crooned

a spring-dawning world
beyond our universe:

new moon, stars, Jupiter, and Mars.
His words are not lost on me;

you were never lost to me—
we are made for another world.

SLOW SORROW

I only saw the crushed shell,
  its body surely the strength
    of another's now. Every
      day I stepped over the crushed.
    The sun was never just bright,
  just right, until today. I saw it—
all the snails had gathered
  in the night and marched around
    the shell like a people marching
      around the city wall
        for six days, and today, the
      sun shone down after a
    somber douse of rain. Now
  encircling the shattered shell
an afterglow,
  luminescent halos
    unsure of their allegros.
      Just when I believe the world
        is too lost in thought
          to cease their march and witness
        the rended, I see not every
      living creature is. On day
    seven, their grief falls slowly,
  restfully, without a shout.

SANCTUARY

If the sun has a dress,
Gloria borrows it: bright yellow
and a matching hat with yellow sequins.

She sits in the pew outside of the sanctuary.
While others smile a faint hello when I enter the church,
she cheers, "You're here, you're here, you're here!"

She clenches my hand and says,
"I'm glad you're here.
Your smile makes me happy."

"I think she's an angel," I whisper to my husband
when we enter the sanctuary.
She sees me when I don't want to be seen,

but need to be seen. At communion,
Gloria is the last to shuffle to the front
for the bread and the cup.

She grabs two of the bread and two of the cup,
and I smile, wondering if her stomach is empty,
but no—she sees what needs to be seen.

In the back row is David, her friend
just released from the hospital.
He cups his hands as she places the Elements.

This body,
broken for you:
taste and see.

DEAR WOMAN WITH A BLACK FOX-DOG

She who lives in the vastness of brush, of once-green life turning to
tumbleweeds, of rattlesnakes, of sticker weeds.
Address Unknown

San Diego, California

Dear Woman with a black fox-dog,
    I pass you every morning.
    A slow-walking second-hand
    vendor with your plastic bag,
    leashed black fox-dog, plaid jacket,
    and beige ballcap, you walk
    the path—a side-glanced pretender—
    of another's life moving
    from front door to sidewalk to
    trash bin to car door to
    repeat, repeat, repeat.

You nudge up your sleeve cuff to
catch the time on your wrist. Who,
I wonder, is expecting you?
There is no record of your mark.
Only the dew betrays your
candor where you sideslip
from the sidewalk to the grass,
only pawprints stain the sidewalk.
Then you emerge with a book
clenched closely to your chest,

and then I understand the
deprivation of sensation
and imagination:
invisibility hoping
visibility. Even

the snail's trail is iridescent
on the electrical box
you sit on each morning to
rest your legs. This is a poem
about you, but really, it is verse

on keening nearsighted
and farsighted. I have never
mistaken your outline for
another—"Hello," says a voice,
and I almost miss you come alive.
Your almost frozen gate and
sun-doused face stretched thin
gives way to cordial greetings.
"Good morning,"
I say, and you shuffle on.

I wish to tell you, neighbor—
I, too, walk alone from front door
to sidewalk and repeat, repeat,
repeat, trying to enter
a palace of imagination
where every life I have faced
touches and coalesces;
I have been expecting you, neighbor,
and your hello is just what
I have been waiting to hear.
Regards,

I, who live across the road from you.

Bell Bluff Avenue
San Diego, California

MATH AND MERCY OVER TEN SECONDS

Two walk out of their front door
together. One waits while one locks the door.
Then they carry on, and that is their story.

It is the first time two have walked out
as one, and not one-by-one, throughout each day
with their third. This third was not their flesh—

not as we think of flesh—giggling, hand reaching,
a sum of how one plus one bears
a newborn from two. This third was a dog,

whose fifteen years was their newborn
created by two. For so many seasons,
the two nursed this third, one-by-one

through his old age until the fourth season
dawned, and their newborn was gone.
Sympathy for loss lasts only as long

as one lingers on the loss and
refrains from comparing values, assigning
a scale of numbers to the greater

or the lesser flesh—thus,
equaling the sum of mercy.
There are infinite testimonies:

a combat veteran, a child psychologist
whose Greater Power accounts
for what is unspoken but witnessed.

5:29 P.M. ON JACKSON DRIVE

A grandfather
  with hair so silver
and a bald spot so shiny,
  I can't look beyond him
pushing
  a black double-stroller
of newborn twins.

On this day,
  when retaliation is promised
throughout the world,
  is a grand-
father stooping low,
  whispering, gently
pushing
  the powerless
with the loudest
  cry
as the sun sets.

I wonder if they hear
  his lullaby.

TO THE UNLIKELIEST

To the bubbles—
> You are beauty on an eight-lane road: glossy, round sheens of
> pink and blue tumbling across gray lanes, hope-fully upward,
> dodging passers-through.

To the blackbirds—
> You are marvel on an overpass: teeming hundreds, swift and
> shifting as a wave, entrancing me into your tempest, into
> your enclave.

To the butterflies—
> You are wonder above alfalfa fields: curtsying your pair,
> a ballet in air, all clothed in white, fluttering above the grass
> tipped with purple fare.

To the white heron—
> You are splendor perched in the crosswalk: Shiver away your
> translucent marble yoke, stretch your neck, unbend your
> smoke-blue legs, and carry forth without your cloak.

For whom were you boasting
in the unlikeliest of places
creation's cadence and unlikely graces?

COUNTING STARS

A woman, childlike, sits with her caretaker-mom at the mall.
My life could be hers; her life could be mine:
Both the same age, yet life has forced us each offbeat.

How are you still here? my physical therapist asked me the day before.
Blood could not reach my brain's left side,
and bursts of blackouts numbed me to the gravity of life.

At the mall, a singer echoes a melodic *life force*,
and grief slow-dances down my cheeks—
only my sunglasses to cover.

When the woman's mom disappears in a store, she stands up,
steps wide side-to-side, and claps like a child to the living rhythm
we all hear but silence behind pretend.

The mandolin's pizzicato glitters like stars tossed
high into the sky. Is she a star? a refraction falling
like crushed glitter? She twirls in circles with

    her purple-tipped blonde hair,
    her Hello Kitty tattoo, and
    her HELLO HAPPY t-shirt

because everyone is watching.
And when the song ends, everyone claps—
    what   life   force.

FELT DARKNESS

I see you
walk out the black screen door
with your Husky. Just
like I saw you
with a pregnant belly.

I see you
with your Husky. Just
like I saw you
with a stroller.

I see you
with your Husky and Husky puppy. Just
like I saw you
without a stroller.

I see you, still,
neighbor,
enduring.

BLESSED IS SHE

Of those quiet streets my husband and I walked before the sun
reached its height, I had already written
a backstory. Of all the layered lives I

imagined behind the cobblestone paths, wrought-iron gates,
and flower boxes, yours I could not conceive.
A white fence restrained my mental trespassing.

On the curb each Saturday morning in July, boxes.
Losses left outside the Cape Cod house,
picturesque by Marine Street beach—

> Free: Forty piano compositions by Frédéric Chopin.
> Compositions begin with *Prelude* and end in *Funeral March*,
> interspersed with a *Waltz*, *Fantasie-Impromptu*, a *Ballade*.

> Free: Two volumes of *Lieder-Schatz, treasure songs*
> encased in ox-blood red leather.
> *True love* penciled over *3. Treue Liebe.*

> Free: Leather-bound French literature
> with *Martha Herrick 1906* inscribed.
> *Though it be but little; it be fierce*, penned inside.

> Free: Indoor house plants in terracotta pots.
> "But we do not have the right sunlight,"
> my husband said, "to keep them alive."

Transfixed by each recent curb offering,
we combed through book after book while neighbors
bellowed *America, the Beautiful*

and marched down the street, embellished in red, white,
and blue. A year had passed of isolating,
and perhaps I was seeking another

life story to dream as we gathered your
discarded artifacts, unaware of your story unfolding
before us, unaware of our parallels—

Free: blank baby book.

I confess, I am in the habit of naming
inanimate objects, of attributing complex inner lives
to unspeakable beings. To you, I'll do neither.

Witness

"The most enduring hymns are born in the silences of the soul, and nothing must be allowed to intrude while they are being framed into language."
—Fanny J. Crosby, *Memories of Eighty Years*

MEMENTO

I played "How It Ends" from *Little Miss Sunshine*
   as we passed the cypress trees into Rome.
Fitting, us chasing an otherworld we pined.
   Beneath my feet, cobbled volcanic stone
throbbed my step an endless night. Riven
   stones with ashen edges like my memories.

How much we live on dispersed memories
   and undulating shadows. We sought sunshine
in St. Peter's Basilica's half-light. Riven,
   we murmured, "Where is The Light?" in Rome.
We traced hand-hewn stones for the cornerstone,
   studying Michelangelo's pined

Pietà where Mary held lifeless Christ's body, heart-pined.
   Truer still, Christ holds mine, and the memories
of me weeping inside St. Peter's stone-
   lined bathroom. The slivered sunshine
crowned a hazy cloud of dew over Rome,
   while my spasming frame writhed a riven

shock. From head to toe, I applied my riven
   body with Icy-Hot. An outer balm, I pined
it so: pierce these heavy-laden bones in Rome.
   Wintergreen—the redolence of Rome's memories,
of wincing the worn hem of sunshine,
   of thrashing for Christ's marbled hand in stone,

of assaying the Spanish Steps for a headstone.
   What odes were penned by the lung-riven
and taken up by nightingales? The sunshine

41

breaks dew "Away! away! for I will fly to thee."[2] Pine,
save the chorus, weep the memories,
    and descend the steps of gold-gilded Rome—

such pangs are shadows atoned in a land we'll roam.
    Soon and very soon, the lifeless in marble stone
returns the Bright Morning Star and ash-heaped memories
    scatter—adorned verse, its meter unriven:
Glory peals through the cypress trees, pining
    my lowly tabernacle lift to the sunshine.

Homeward, the turbulence breathes us on, rivening
    the weight of *why*. You've always known, always pined
the end: a garden, an exile homed, sunshine.

2. Keats, "Ode to a Nightingale," stanza 4.

FOR US, A CHORUS

The bowl in my hand, his lifeless body
thrown to the rocks of a five-inch sea,

I was unraveled by Romeo's death,
and it was the night of your twenty-fifth.

You took the bowl, his midnight fins blazing
and buried him, fitting.

He wouldn't be alone? I pleaded his
significance—remember each Christmas?

How he rode home buckled in my passenger seat
and teamed as I read Shakespeare's love defeat?

Who mused this beta tragedy
foreshadowing ours the years following?

The loyal man kneeling,
my slipped body reeling,

a lofty chorus high above us—
tragedy's quiet soliloquies.

BARE

After Andrew Wyeth's Christina's World *(1948)*

Had I known that to write my foreground, I
    must leave the farmland—I would have weighed
my whispers to the heights, my verse sung nigh,
    while tempest wrestled the barbed wire stayed.

Dressed for church but let out to pasture—
    a wounded animal left to hope alone
against the marred sun while the sky smoldered—
    I knuckled, straining my cerebrum home:

      Where the orange poppies cleave the split skin,
        the grape hyacinths jockey the sapped grass,
      the oxblood tulips upheave their silk chin,
        the blazing heads of wheat pierce forth. *Alas,*

let the glory of the dying lie bare,
    shadowing the shadow, rooted to the ground.

NIGHT FLOWER

Magnolias bloom here
  in winter,
  and back home,
while the sun hangs low,
  they wait
  for field corn's
bittersweet cream
  to bleed out
  in the cold,
while I wait
  another foggy night
  for star sparks
to rust the magnolias'
  leather petals
  a burnt ochre,
while Twilight rides
  on the moon's clouds,
while the red-shouldered
  hawk circles round
  and round,
witnessing
  this kindling edge.

ONE HUNDRED WORDS OF SOLITUDE

I retrace the familiar while lying on the table
in the doctor's office each week. This room
has eleven ceiling tiles: square and white.

A different doctor, a different retracing,
but still familiar. Twelve ceiling tiles:
rectangle and ivory.

A new room this day. Rare: finger-paintings
with primary colors—palm trees, sun—
atop square and white.

I study the rare.
Hundreds of doctors' appointments. Retracing
hundreds of solitudes.

But the prayers for a song
in the night to come
in the night, comes.

Echoes of mercy, whispers of love.[3]
Keeping time, I retrace the chorused Hope.
Watching and waiting, I look above.

3. Crosby, "Blessed Assurance," 317.

SPRINGTIME: TWO SANTAS IN STREET CLOTHES IN A DOCTOR'S WAITING ROOM

Santa One: "Beard—natural. You?"
Santa Two: "Natural."

Santa One: "The conference in March?"
Santa Two: "Magical."

Santa One: "Your suit—polyester? And your belt—black leather?"
Santa Two: "Rayon suit, black leather belt."

A pause in disbelief.

Shifting their bellies, they pull out their IDs.
"The North Pole," they both laugh.

I am the only other one in the chamber
for the wishful—the waiting room.

"What do you want for Christmas, little lady?"

But they do not ask.

"A new body," I would say.

"Megan," the nurse calls,
and I close my book, *The Curious Reader.*

My every step is wince-filled,
yet it is not I who wonders over their magic,

it is they who wonder the mystery of my step—
my falter across the linoleum floor,

like a cumbersome carol
wished to another.

THE SKY ABOVE MY BED

The sky above my bed
is nine feet high and in moments of wonder,
I stand with my feet cratered on the bed
and I can palm the plastered clouds, the mini T-rex. Is this
what dreams are made of?

For nine weeks, I have laid here in hours of three,
in hopes that these hours might seal what my spine's dura feels:
bruised beyond these words by a drunk driver.
At night, my husband reads the biographies of saints,
and we question how they held on.

For it has taken nine weeks, yet one afternoon, I see it:
the robin's robust body takes flight. Or
do its claws grip the ground? And
have I glimpsed its attempt? Now I see another,
a mourning dove, struggling mid-flight.

The ceiling clouds obscure its body. Or
is the obscurity its color
too light to see? When I was nine,
I found a robin's blue freckled egg,
its backside dented, that had fallen from the juniper tree

outside my bedroom window.
I knew of death in animals.
I knew its mama would reject the egg,
just like the stray mama cats would reject the kittens in the milk barn
birthed on the gunny sacks that smelled of my hands.

And now I wonder: How
do the robin and mourning dove endure
the winds? How
does the fledgling, then its wings—how
can it rest upon the invisible?

Now I see—
the robin's attempt,
the mourning dove's flight,
the clouds breaking—
they'll fly away, some glad morning.

BE

In the secret, praise
  what is given. Then be
the calatheas plant
  in the kitchen
that raises its drape,
  lifts its scorched leaves,
unscrolls its foliage,
  and vespers the neon jots
to the lesser light, for
  the lesser is
still light.

ALL, I PRAYED

You cut roses from the garden that withstood—
yellow, saccharin, bursting bright yet folding fast.
The blooms still smelled though their heads bowed low.

Winter overshadowed spring, and all I prayed
for was a glimpse of the sun. The bloom offered
a quick defeat, contrasting your endurance

for these seasons where we become bondservants
to my body's inner irregular rhythm.
The yellow petals clung to the vase as I poured them into the sink.

Even as I did it, I felt pained, but I turned on the garbage disposal.
            Where is the sun?

The saccharine scent of the rose
arose from the sink, and I asked
if I could take it all back:

        winter barraging spring,
        the sun withholding,
        the insipid accusation,

        my body's bindings,
        this broken rhythm,
        the roses' sacrifice.

In the garden, where sunlight may soon
peek through, a bud remains,
and I am awed in wonder:

even roses grow in the shadows,
and when crushed,
they still surrender a scent.

A DREAM IN RESPONSE TO WORDS HANGING IN THE NIGHT AIR

You're a dreamer, you say under the glow
of lamplight that umbrellas the bedroom.
These words said to mirror the soul's cargo,
but I lie, searching ceiling stars, cocooned.

Night plunges to dream: You and me beneath,
swimming the edge of earth's icy waters.
Dream's voice ushers us beyond marbled depths,
where one light downcasts refracting mirrors:

Here is the edge of this eternity.
We heed, is this life a memory we wake
unto—where wracked bones face the heavenly
bodies—or are heaven's waters the first wake?

At next day's light, you say, *Winter is thawing.*
Wait for the waking tide—spring is coming.

WORDS TOO FEW: IT IS WELL

A bouquet of blooms on a day of good health.
  The hours usher us
to surrender to the idles of health.

One flower bows its bloom, and
  the days usher surrender
one by one by one.

I remember petals still
  white, blooms brought low
to the hope of health—bear it no more.

To the hope of it is well:
  I can still smell the fresh bouquet.

COUNTRY MUSIC

on returning home

On this first hour of summer, even the trees sweat sap,
    and KOOL105 plays every Oldie in tempo
with an inner beat I once embodied
    but haven't swayed to in years.

The cornfield sounds my subconscious—
    ditch water hiccupping down the row,
disappearing between stalks like a whisper
    in a landspout caught up in the sky.

Later, the sky lights up a paparazzi shower,
    like fallen stars sprouting from ground to sky to onion fields
with lightning-sharp whips. I count *one, two, three,*
    and thunder peals outside my window at the farmhouse.

Less than a mile away, I say
    as the scent of bruised onions pervades.

Boom-Boom
    the hail cannons's sonic shock pierce
    black clouds, weakening frozen formations—
    me.
Boom-Boom

I pray for the cicadas's *sugar-sugar-sugar*
    shrill. *Only six more weeks of this,*
my dad would say. Six more weeks
    until the living dies by season, not by assault.

Till then, I will harvest the memories.

REMEMBER WHEN

we danced.
  you held up my body,
swaying our steps,

and if they could see
  our spontaneous sway,
they would question

the rhythm: is that
  dancing? this I know,
meter fills these bones,

a shivering cry
  to my ache:
listen

to the music—
  remember when
before the pain,

and remember when
  we're promised
there will be no pain.

MY PRAYER VOICE

Pull this dura tight

and tune it like the lyre.

Strum me in D-minor—

grief's major key—

and I will quake,

straining for high C

in the shadow.

THE NURSERY

The nursery is where we dream,
tiptoeing around the workers as they make their morning rounds,
to see our daydreams in nature's most honest dyes.

You make it there first and motion me to come over.
You cradle its head in the palm of your hand.
Beautiful, you say.

> The week prior, we had walked along cracks in the asphalt
> hiking trail near our condo, noting the beauty of brown
> bushels of tumbleweeds because we were still clinging
> to that small root of home
>
> when life was impregnated with turnings of resplendent
> swatches of hues—pinks and blues to greens to yellows and
> oranges; when morning dustings cloaked the familiar i
> n white that shook itself free by lunchtime.
>
> The trail had carved a path between dormant life that waited
> for the next season, but we stayed on ours. And like a yawn
> stalls time as if to say, *slow down, I need just one more breath*
> *to make it through*, I grab your hand on the trail and say,
> *I need just one more breath.*
>
> And out of a crack in the asphalt was a twiggy weed, gray,
> looking like it could be crushed. I bent to hold the tiny
> purple flower growing from the deceased. I had wanted to
> whisper: *Of all the dead, you are the only color.*

Is this what you've dreamt of? you ask me at the nursery, still
cradling the delicate head. I bring my hand beneath yours, and the
soft pink, silky petals give way into our hands.
It is, I say, and name her Opal, just like I name all of our living matters.

Two dreams have spoken honestly to me in the night:
I want to touch a memory in you.
But these are not memories. These are night wishes rooted deep
with sunlight, water, and air cutoff.

Because sometimes the hardest to imagine comes in the color of
night, with the most profound sensation, yet it's the hardest
to reach. So I reach for you, hoping to grab you and ask,
Can what's been undone be done?

Light

"Color directly influences the soul.
Color is the keyboard, the eyes are the hammers,
the soul is the piano with many strings."
—Wassily Kandinsky, *Concerning the Spiritual in Art*

PRISON'S PRISM

the synchronicity of pain
is my prison's prism, and
I am a sacred lonely.
it stitches me in
my concrete corset
with its spellbound hold.
but you see the color, and I
wear the corset and ache in witness:
to feel wing's shadow,
to see hue in night,
for what is color but made in darkness
and syncopated but refrain?

your needle hems a gold-
dusted chorus—faint,

the weaning of life to the meaning
of daynight's dyes: from dust
to gold to life-forged light,
my glory-made sight.

HYMNED

We shall wake, to weep no more,[4]
are the final lines of worship, when pain
inches up my spine like a caterpillar
with serrated blades striating its back.

It is no monarch inching out,
my eyes awash with tears so dense
I only feel the hand grab mine,
then my husband's arm lead me out.

Outside, the dry heat rushes
to my crackling chrysalis,
and the green wild parrots
with blazoned red heads

squawk a wild cacophony above us.
In the car, you whisper,
you're safe. Then a
knock-knock hits my window,

and I flinch at the presence
of someone else watching my caving.
It is that first hand knocking,
her tears a whisper as I open the door.

Do words matter? As a poet,
I say yes. But a hug—
a muted refrain—
is worship.

4. Crosby, "The Bright Forever," stanza 2.

IMAGINE A BIRD

I comb through the familiar
knots at the nape of my neck

and trill my fingers in the wind,
goodbying every blond strand,

wishing them anew,
and ruminating on this season

that begins with a wooly blanket of fog
and ends with a pink veil of sunlight—

a season where I wonder if it's spring or fall—
                    I live so close to that veil.

                    I imagine a bird—a wren afresh
into nesting, gathering one invisible strand

of blond in its beak, flying to its knobby perch,
and weaving the strand through twigs,

clay mud, and color-leeched leaves.
If I cannot rebuild with what I relinquish,

I reckon you, wren, are readying your nest
with a restless joy.

A SUMMARY OF MERCY

I expected crow's feet first
   from squinting to understand
the red script on weakness.
      But my smile lines are the first
to form, the first impression
   left of me grasping for life.

WHILE I WAKE

Glimmer Spiel

Are
butterflies image
bearers
of
angels
descending?

And the breeze,
cool on a summer day,
is You whispering,
this is temporal,
this wayfaring
that engulfs you.

Only Caterpillars Crawl With Singular Aim

each day marked internally by dye
not of their own choosing.
Someday—when,

I do not know—but I will see
life lifted high, this prism butterfly
emerge glorified. And I will see

each glory a wonder of curation,
a flash of dawning,
a new creation.

When Eternity Began

Like after the rainstorm,
when I found a white butterfly
in my jeans pocket

after crawling
through milkweed.

Only looking back
do I live
in such astonishment.

*"Fly, Butterfly," my mom wrote in a note to me at the onset of my
illness. These poems are me taking flight, Mom.*

FLED IS THAT MUSIC:—DO I WAKE OR SLEEP?[5]

a golden shovel after John Keats' "Ode to a Nightingale"

From the fiery furnace, I fled
    on the wings of whispers. Is
bravato the young bird trilling for a voice that
    ceases with dawn? Then may the hopeful's music
lean upon the whole-note rest to do
    its promise: clear the dross, take the whisper I
wing nigh, and wake
    the shut-in with cracked bells or
lilt the metronomed heart with sweet-toned sleep.

5. Keats, "Ode to a Nightingale," stanza 8.

HOMEGOING

seventh-grade hallway
red beanbag in the basement
kitchen sinks
gray-distressed hutch
language Arts class
kitchen dishwashers
middle couch cushion
Eaton Middle School curb
front pew singing "How Great Thou Art"
red school locker
World Market aisle
toolshed
cruise ship balcony
writing desk (legions)
hallways
left couch cushion
bathroom doorway
brown corduroy chair
392 and 257 stoplight
dining room table (countless)
high school choir room
picture window
airplane window (as many as stars)

…but heaven
has gained
half more
its joys

6. Bonar, *The Diary and Life of Andrew Bonar.*

I PRAY THIS

I pray this
  powdery-blue envelope
meets you
  with little tinge
and lesser scuff
  from credit card offers,
energy bills,
  mortgage payments,
or coupon fliers.

Let no rain stain
  nor fester
bluer blisters—
  more than you already bear.

As you slide your finger
  beneath the fold,
releasing the licked bond,
  may it give and give
without blood,
  freeing the sting of
goodbye.

GLORY, US

saints of thunder and night, saints' souls plundered for light—

bend low, and give Me your tears.
I have come to glory: this life, this body
turned upside-down is right-side-up,
right by my side, kept,
your hand cupped
in My palm, I'll draw you up.

your brokenness is worth redeeming, My brokenness is your beauty.

we grasp Your hand reaching near,
and though we fear,
You draw us to the Maker's mirror:

your surrender, My glory | My glory, your splendor

EUPHONY

The fire stolen to light humanity
  from dust to clay to bone to flesh: *woe*, gods.
To mold life, the titan-god oracled
  dust-man and cast the fates as life-givers.

This tainted hymn of glory smolders so:
  Hallowed be, hallowed be, hallow-
Ears have perceived what lips unclean utter
  most. The mythic pursuit to echo life.

Elohim whispers *Messiah* above.
  Woe! The totality of history ignites.
I hold euphony, a six-winged seraph
  sounding a cicada rattle to my lips:

  holy, holy, holy, holy, holy

Lips are atoned at the uttermost thought—*YHWH*.
  Dust-man is lifted from his calloused heart,
Chavah is raised from shame to her name: *Eve*.
  The transfigured weep: *Hallelujah, hallelujah, hallelujah*

MIRRORED & MAGNIFIED

In the field of dry corn rows, I stand, carrying a wait-less weight

of these silent moments before harvest comes to be. When

the green tips of corn leaves turn a piercing brown, when

the leaves' once-pulsing veins emerge black, branded, when

the husk hug tighter the ear of corn to envelop the kernels, when

the angel-hair silk turns brittle, when

the stalk hollows, when

the tassel bows

under the weight

of fall.

I am brought low under the wait—the vanes of when

and wind, the night-dusk tugging the ear

infernal, the broken hallowed

stalk, the buckling tassel,

the white-haired angel,

the arresting moments

of bowing,

of piercing,

of silence,

of weightlessness,

of being

fully seen.

EN PLEIN AIR

I once could walk to the lake's center,
  its bed wrinkled like the ravines
of a ninety-year-old soul. Emptied
  at its depths, I sat—at the feet—and asked
for all of this to mean something, something
  more than just no crop-life for the year,
more decay of the living. Because I've witnessed it
  more than once—the lilies toiling and spinning,
toiling, not from their own affliction.

En plein air, I paint the lake outstretched,
  brimming behind me. I brush the cairns like hay bales:
the blazing bush extinguished viridescent,
  the creeks quivering serene, my mom's rose seed
that grew into an Elm tree (God knew
  we would need the shade) budding its first red rose.

Still I lie, being
  taken from the bed of shoulders,
looking at all that lies behind,
  and I then rise—spinning,
                    spinning,
                          spinning
                               with light.

THE ONE WHO SEES

In the beginning was water and my pink and white gingham dress.

We were chasing Muffin, my older sister's cat, by the creek that ran behind the milk barn near the sheep corral, and I was trailing behind my siblings. Before crossing the bridge, I broke away to the hundred-year-old cottonwood tree. Peering up into its canopy of chattering leaves that shimmied in the breeze, I ran my fingers over its scaly bark. An owl lived high in this tree, and though I had never seen him, I had heard him and knew he was there.

I hopped down the emerald bank to the creek swirling at the roots of the cottonwood. Barn swallows darted out from under the bridge, then scattered high in the cumulous-filled sky. I stepped closer to the murky waters while holding my dress from the muddy banks, curious about the leaves, as big as my cheeks, being drawn down in the small whirlpool.

Megan! I heard. Then I slipped from the bank and went under, unable to swim.

≈

In elementary school, my swim coach would yell at me to jump off the diving board while he would wade in the deep. My toes would curl over the edge of the board, me fearful, believing that the stronger the grip, the safer the jump.

I'll catch you, he would say.

I would jump and he would pull back, perhaps thinking that the best way to learn how to swim was to paddle as though your life depended on it. But I would struggle in the aqua deep while he would throw a buoy and pull me to the side of the pool.

In middle school, I would be on an innertube at the lake, surrounded with cottonwoods, on the west side of the family farm that fed into our creek. My oldest brother would be pulling me on a jet ski when, suddenly, a small wake would flip me into the forest-green water and the rope would tangle around my neck.

When I would float to the surface—fine, but spooked—my brother would gasp, *Your neck!* and tow me to shore. The rope burn, hot and sticky, would encircle my neck and reach up to my chin. My family would panic, unbuckle my life jacket, and make me rest on the marshy banks in the shade of the cottonwood trees.

≈

I don't remember when I learned to swim. I only remember when I was saved.

Because in my beginning was someone hovering above the face of the deep. I could hear him—he called me by name—though I couldn't see him.

For under the creek waters that day, my eyes met another: my oldest brother's hand illuminated white under the water. He drew me from the water and set my feet on solid ground.

For there has always been One who has moved across the waters, trading life for life, plunging the depths, drawing me, and raising me to new heights. My frame, with the former gingham dress that once clung to me, fell in pink droplets, and I have been clothed in white ever since. On that eternal day, when I have crossed the banks and am at His shore of crystalline waters, when I am nearer to His feet—no longer revering from afar but swallowed up with the lapping tide, face lifted and cradled in soft hands—He will see me, behold me, and say, *Megan! Good, I found you.*

Note

"My First Still Life" was originally featured on July 4, 2023 on *The Habit Podcast* with Jonathan Rogers under a longer title: *Impressions of a Hometown*. The piece consisted of two parts: the first part included a prose introduction detailing an annual gathering in my small agricultural hometown of Eaton, Colorado. The second part of the piece consisted of the poem, "My First Still Life," which opens this poetry collection.

Impressions of a Hometown
By Megan (Cozzens) Huwa

On February 11, 2023, the townsfolk of Eaton, Colorado paid $25 a ticket to gather in the Evangelical Free Church and hear the Pioneer Society of Eaton tell a story they already knew.

It's the story shared over barbed wire fences while moving cattle, over early morning coffee, after changing the first head of water, between rolled-down driver's-side pickup windows, and beside the grain elevator.

My oldest brother, the vice-president of the society and the fifth generation on the Cozzens family farm, retold the story of the Cozzens family, updating the town's oral repository with farm and family photos and the changing landscape of agriculture.

My family's story is just one of many in my hometown, for Eaton beats with the hearts of pioneers—their stories and their perseverance in the face of storms that surmount with every passing season.

Ask me for a glimpse of Eden, and I offer you the corner of two county roads intersecting where part of the Cozzens family farm homesteaded at the turn of the 20th century.

Ask me for a glimpse of the fall of Eden, and I offer this impression: a poem of my father, the patriarch of the Cozzens family farm. This is the artistry of farm towns. This is "My First Still Life."

Bibliography

Bonar, Andrew. *The Diary and Life of Andrew A. Bonar*. Edited by Marjory Bonar. East Peoria, IL: The Benner of Truth Trust, 2018. First published 1893.

Crosby, Fanny J. "Blessed Assurance, Jesus is Mine." *Hymns for the Living Church*. Carol Stream, IL: Hope, 1984.

———. "The Bright Forever." Hymnary, June 27, 2025. https://hymnary.org/text/breaking_through_the_clouds_that_gather

———. *Memories of Eighty Years*. Disability History Museum. Boston: James H. Earle & Company, 1906. https://www.disabilitymuseum.org/dhm/lib/detail.html?id=1653&&print=1&&page=41.

———. "Rescue the Perishing." *Hymns for the Living Church*. Carol Stream, IL: Hope, 1984.

Kandinsky, Wassily. *Concerning the Spiritual in Art*. Translated by M.T.H. Sadler. 1914. Reprint, Constable and Company Limited. New York, NY: Dover, 1977.

Keats, John. "Ode to a Nightingale." The Poetry Foundation, April 1, 2025. https://www.poetryfoundation.org/poems/44479/ode-to-a-nightingale.

9798385255214